SIZES AND SHAPES

Illustrated by the Disney Storybook Artists

© 2010 Disney Enterprises, Inc. All Rights Reserved.

This publication may not be reproduced in whole or in part by any means whatsoever
without written permission from the copyright owners. Permission is never granted for commercial purposes.
Published by Louis Weber, C.E.O., Publications International, Ltd., 7373 North Cicero Avenue, Lincolnwood, Illinois 60712
Ground Floor, 59 Gloucester Place, London W1U 8JJ

Customer Service: 1-800-595-8484 or customer_service@pilbooks.com

www.pilbooks.com

p i kids is a registered trademark of Publications International, Ltd.

8 7 6 5 4 3 2 1

Manufactured in China.

ISBN-13: 978-1-4508-0288-8   ISBN-10: 1-4508-0288-5

Hello, there! Today we're going to look inside and outside the Clubhouse for things of different shapes and sizes.

First, we need to get outside. I see three doors. Each of them is a different shape. What shapes do you see?

To get outside the Clubhouse, we need to use the door that is shaped like a rectangle. Can you spot the rectangle? Hot dog!

Now we're outside, and the whole gang has joined us! Say hello to Pluto, Goofy, Minnie, Daisy, and Donald.

For our size and shape adventure, we'll need a way to get around. Maybe Toodles can help us out. Oh, Toodles!

What shape is Toodles's screen? That's right, it's a circle!

Hot dog! Toodles has a balloon for us to ride in. Most balloons are circles, just like Toodles. But not this hot-air balloon. What is our balloon shaped like?

Up, up, and away! We're flying high in
the air, and we can see for miles and miles.
Who do you see playing golf?
Can you spot any shapes below our
balloon? How many triangles do you see?

Now we're back at the Clubhouse. Let's give Daisy a hand in the kitchen. And let's look for things that are round, like circles and ovals.

Do you see any round things in the kitchen? I'll give you a hint — tick-tock.

Do you see any food that is round?

We don't only have to look for shapes. We can also look for things of different sizes. Which bowl is bigger? Which one is smaller?

We can find things that are different sizes outside, too.

Take a look at those hills. They all look pretty big, right?

But some of the hills are bigger, or taller, than other hills.

Which hill is the tallest? Which one is the shortest?

Those hills aren't the only tall and big things outside.

Take this cliff, for example. Hot dog, is it high! It's much higher than me. It's a good thing I brought a climbing rope.

Which bush is bigger?

And look over there at those trees. Are they all the same size? Which tree is the biggest? Which tree is the smallest?

Small things can be different shapes and sizes, too. Let's visit Minnie in her garden, and you'll see what I mean.

Look at those three sunflowers. They're not big like trees and hills, are they? But one of them is taller than the rest. Which one is the tallest? Which sunflower is the shortest?

One last size game, and then
we'll go on a different adventure.
Which rock is the biggest?
Which one is the smallest?
Good work! You're a super
shaper and sizer. See you next time!